DATE DUE

NOV 19 1997	APR 23 2007	
DEC 10 1997	MAY 21 2007	
JUN 9 1999	JUL 20 2009	
AUG 28 2002	APR 26 2010	
SEP 11 2002	FEB 22 2012	
JUN 21 2004	SEP 30 2013	
JUL 06 2004		
AUG 17 2005	OCT 21 2013	
AUG 31 2005		
APR 19 2006	AUG 17 2016	
MAY 01 2006		

LET'S INVESTIGATE SCIENCE

Natural Resources

LET'S INVESTIGATE SCIENCE
Natural Resources

Robin Kerrod

Illustrated by Ted Evans

MARSHALL CAVENDISH
NEW YORK · LONDON · TORONTO · SYDNEY

Library Edition Published 1994

© Marshall Cavendish Corporation 1994

Published by Marshall Cavendish Corporation
2415 Jerusalem Avenue
PO Box 587
North Bellmore
New York 11710

Series created by Graham Beehag Book Design

Library of Congress Cataloging-in-Publication Data

Kerrod, Robin.
    Natural Resources / Robin Kerrod; llustrated by Ted Evans.
    p. cm. -- (Let's investigate science)
    Includes index.
    ISBN 1-85435-628-3   ISBN 1-85435-688-7 (set)
    1. Earth sciences--Juvenile literature. 2. Natural resources--
Juvenile literature.
    [1. Earth sciences. 2. Natural resources.]
    I. Evans, Ted ill. II. Title. III. Series: Kerrod, Robin.
    Let's investigate science.
    QE29.K37 1994
    333.79--dc20
                                                              93-46025
                                                              CIP
                                                              AC

Printed and bound in Hong Kong.

Contents

Introduction   7

Chapter 1
Anatomy of the Earth   9
Birth of the Earth   10
The moving surface   12
Building mountains   14
Volcanoes and earthquakes   16
Shaping the land   18
Our watery world   20
The atmosphere   22
Age of the Earth   24

Chapter 2
Mineral Resources   27
Fire rocks   28
Sedimentary rocks   30
Changed rocks   32
Minerals and crystals   34
Ore minerals   36
Minerals galore   38
Mining methods   40

Chapter 3
Energy Resources   43
The fossil fuels   44
Oil and gas   46
Producing oil   48
Coal   50
Nuclear energy   52
Renewable resources   54

Milestones   56
Glossary   57
Answers   60
Further reading   62
Index   63

Introduction

The Earth we live on is a huge ball of rock, covered mainly by water and surrounded by a thin layer of air. It is one of nine planets that circle in space around the Sun. The Sun brings light and warmth to the Earth.

The Sun's light and warmth, and the presence of water and air, make it possible for life to occur on Earth in millions of different forms. There is no life on the other planets of our Solar System, because conditions are not suitable.

The rocks that make up the Earth's crust, or hard outer layer, provide us with most of the materials we need to make the machines, devices, and goods we use in our everyday lives. The rocks and the minerals they contain form our mineral resources.

Most of the materials we use as fuels – oil, coal, and natural gas – are also extracted from the ground. They form our main energy resources.

The first chapter of this book introduces some basic geology (geology is the scientific study of the Earth). The second chapter looks more closely at rocks and minerals and the way we use them. The third chapter concentrates on our energy resources.

You can check your answers to the questions featured throughout this book on pages 60-61.

◄ The island of Hawaii, which was created by volcanoes. This picture taken from space clearly shows the lava flows from the islands huge volcanoes. In the center is Mauna Loa, to the left is Mauna Kea, and at the top is Kilauea.

1

Anatomy of the Earth

◄ This picture taken from space shows the Red Sea between Africa and Arabia. The Red Sea is gradually widening because of movements in the Earth's crust.

Q 1. If north is toward the top of the picture, on which side of the Red Sea is Africa?

▼ 1. View of the Northern Hemisphere (northern half) of the Earth as it would appear from space at a point above the North Pole.
2. View of the Southern Hemisphere (southern half) of the Earth as it would appear from space at a point above the South Pole.

Q 2. By tracing these hemispheres and placing the tracings over graph paper, estimate how much more of the Earth's surface is covered by water than by land.

The Earth was born, along with the Sun and the other planets, thousands of millions of years ago and has changed continually over this period. The forces that brought about changes in the past are still at work today, both inside and outside the planet.

On the inside, movements of the "plates" that make up the outer crust create mountains and trigger off volcanoes and earthquakes. On the outside, relentless attack on the surface rocks by the weather and flowing water gradually wears the rocks down and in time totally transforms the landscape.

Q 3. Like all the planets, the Earth moves in different ways. It spins on its axis like a top, and it circles around the Sun. How long does it take the Earth (A) to spin around once, (B) to circle the Sun once?

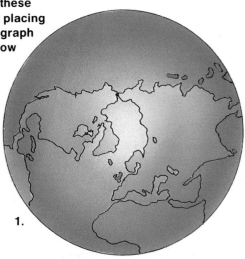

1.

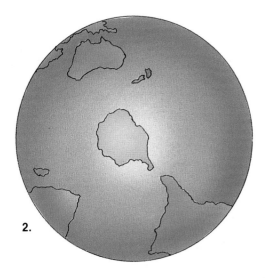

2.

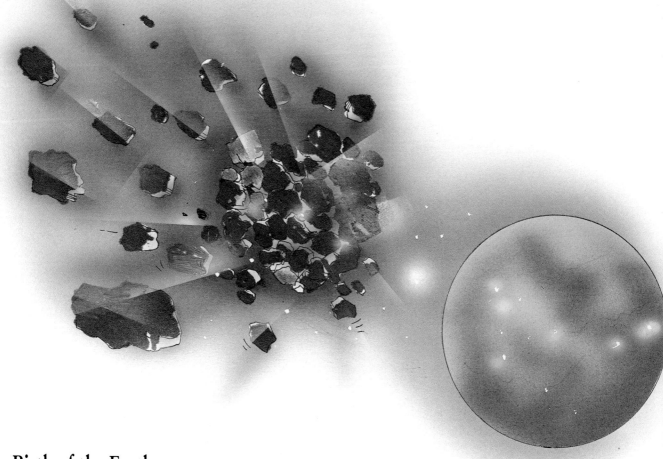

Birth of the Earth

The Earth was born about 5 billion years ago. We believe that at this time the region of space that the Sun, the Earth, and the other planets of our Solar System now occupy was a mass of gas and tiny specks of dust. Such a mass is called a nebula.

Then something caused the gas and dust to start condensing, or coming together. The particles began attracting one another to form larger lumps. In time, the gas and lumps of matter formed into a disk shape, with a bulge in the middle. This bulge eventually became the Sun.

The particles in the outer parts of the disk kept colliding and sticking together, forming bigger and bigger lumps. One of these lumps was the Earth.

Q **1.** What do we call the force that attracts bits of matter to one another?

▲ Billions of years ago lumps of matter came together to form the Earth. Eventually the Earth swept up most of the lumps in the surrounding space. It became very hot, partly because of the collisions it suffered.

Q 2. Why did the collisions cause it to heat up?

A layered Earth

Because of constant collisions and processes taking place inside, the Earth became so hot that it melted. Over millions of years, it slowly cooled down and formed a solid crust. Later still, the oceans formed as water condensed from the clouds and fell as rain.

When the Earth was molten, heavy iron and nickel metal sank to the middle, forming the present core. A deep layer of rocky material formed around the core, making up what is called the mantle. A thin layer on top of the mantle hardened to form the crust, the part of the Earth we are familiar with.

WORKOUT

Using the figures in the diagram, figure out the volume of the Earth in cubic miles (cubic kilometers). If the relative density of the Earth averages 5½, what is the mass of the Earth in tons (tonnes)? The density of water is 62.4 pounds/cubic foot (1 kg/liter).

11

▼ The structure of the Earth today. Only the thin crust is hard. The mantle is plastic, which means that it can flow slowly under pressure. The outer part of the core is liquid, the inner part is solid. The approximate thicknesses of the various layers are given on the diagram.

Q What is the diameter of the Earth?

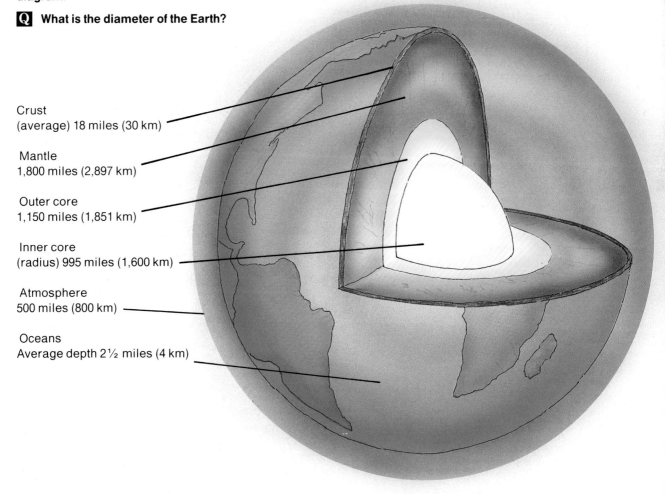

Crust
(average) 18 miles (30 km)

Mantle
1,800 miles (2,897 km)

Outer core
1,150 miles (1,851 km)

Inner core
(radius) 995 miles (1,600 km)

Atmosphere
500 miles (800 km)

Oceans
Average depth 2½ miles (4 km)

The moving surface

If you had a very long tape measure and measured the width of the Atlantic Ocean every year, you would find a strange thing. The Atlantic is getting wider – by about 3 inches (8 cm) a year.

It seems as if the continents of North America and Europe are drifting apart, and in fact they are. This is an example of what is called continental drift.

The person who first put forward the idea of continental drift was a German scientist named Alfred Wegener (1880-1930). Strangely, he was not a geologist but a meteorologist – a weather scientist.

He first put forward the idea of continental drift in 1912, but it did not become widely known until ten years later, and it was not generally accepted until the 1960s.

Theory of plates

Wegener presented evidence that continental drift occurs but couldn't explain why it happens. Geologists can now do so.

Continental drift occurs because the Earth's crust is not rigid all over, but is made up of sections, or "plates," that can move around. The plates are carried along – slowly but surely – by the gradual flow of soft rocks in the upper part of the mantle.

This theory that explains continental drift is known as plate tectonics. It also explains how mountain ranges form (see page 14) and where and why volcanoes and earthquakes occur (see page 16).

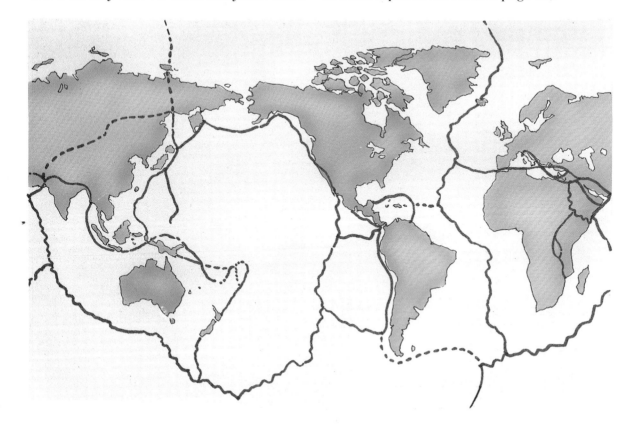

Continents adrift

Applying the theory of continental drift, geologists have figured out what the Earth's surface probably looked like in the past. They calculate that 200 million years ago there was one supercontinent, which they call Pangaea. Gradually it split up into the continents we know today.

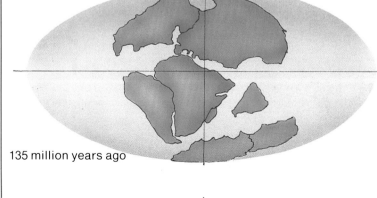

200 million years ago

135 million years ago

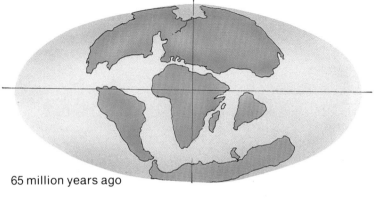

65 million years ago

◄ ◄ This map shows the main plates that make up the Earth's crust. North America and South America sit on separate plates. So do Europe and Africa. Note that there is a plate boundary along the western coast of North America and South America.

Fit the jigsaw

Using tracing paper, trace from an atlas the shape of South America and the shape of Africa. Place the tracing of the western coast of Africa over the tracing of the eastern coast of South America. What do you notice?

Building mountains

The plates that carry the continents are all moving in different directions. In places, plates meet head-on. They push against one another with enormous force, and this causes the land in between to wrinkle and buckle and rise. The result is a mountain range.

The Alps in Europe were formed when the plate carrying Africa collided with the one carrying Europe and Asia. The Himalayas, the highest mountains on Earth, were formed when the plate carrying India collided with the Eurasian plate.

Q **1.** What is the highest Himalayan mountain? About how high is it in miles (kilometers)?

North American mountains

The map opposite shows the main mountain ranges of North America. In the west are long parallel ranges known as the Cordilleras. In the east are the Appalachians.

The Cordilleras were formed less than 140 million years ago as a result of collision between the spreading Pacific floor and the North American plate.

The Eastern Cordilleras, better known as the Rocky Mountains, run down the whole continent, from Alaska into Mexico, a distance of more than 3,0⁰ miles (5,000 km). Nearer the coas⸱ Western Cordilleras, which inclu⸱ Alaska, Coast, Cascade, and ⸱ Nevada ranges. In between the E⸱ and Western Cordilleras ⸱ an inte⸱ tane ("between-mountain"⸱ ⸱⸱ plateaus, such as the Co⸱⸱ and vast basins, such as the ⸱

Q **2.** The highest peak i⸱ ie⸱ in the Alaska Range. 20.⸱0 feet (6,194 mete⸱ na⸱e?

▼ In some oceans, new plate material is forming at an ocean ridge. From the ridge the plates travel east and west. This is called sea-floor spreading. When the ocean plate meets a plate carrying a continent, the pressures that are set up force the land to buckle into a mountain range. The Andes Mountains i⸱ ⸱ ⸱ ⸱ ⸱ were formed in this way.

The ocean plate slides unde⸱ continental plate, and friction b⸱ ⸱ ⸱ ⸱ ⸱ causes them to melt. Sometim⸱⸱ ⸱ t⸱ ⸱ ock forces its way to the surface, ⸱⸱⸱ ⸱an es.

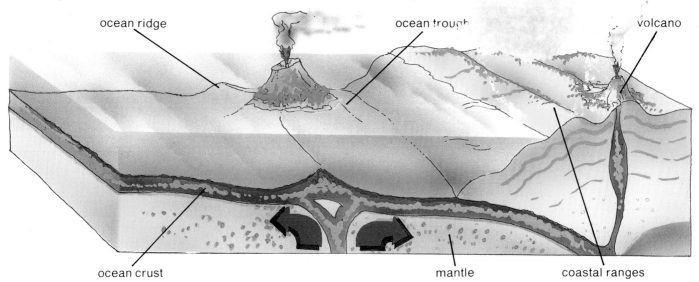

ocean ridge   ocean trough   volcano

ocean crust   mantle   coastal ranges

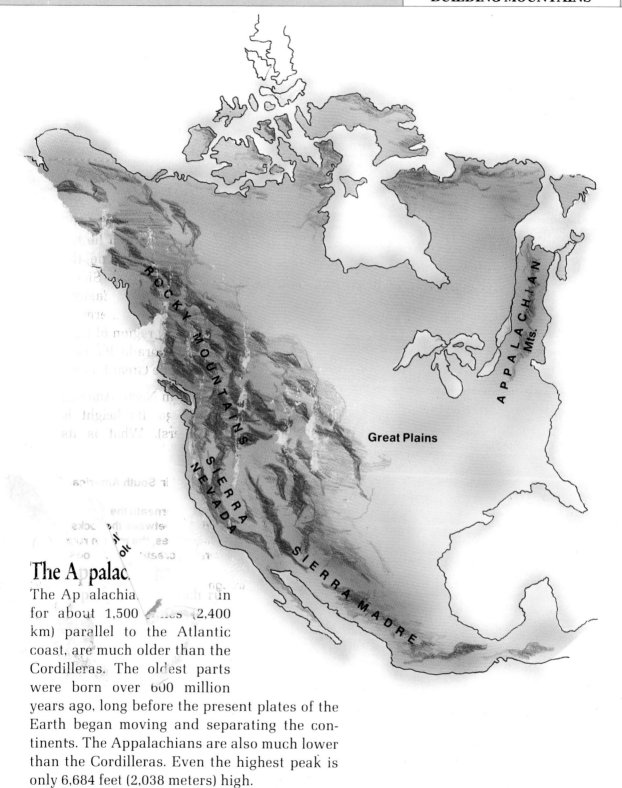

ROCKY MOUNTAINS

SIERRA NEVADA

SIERRA MADRE

APPALACHIAN Mts.

Great Plains

The Appalac

The Appalachia... run for about 1,500 miles (2,400 km) parallel to the Atlantic coast, are much older than the Cordilleras. The oldest parts were born over 600 million years ago, long before the present plates of the Earth began moving and separating the continents. The Appalachians are also much lower than the Cordilleras. Even the highest peak is only 6,684 feet (2,038 meters) high.

Q What is its name?

Volcanoes and earthquakes

Volcanoes occur when molten rock, or magma, in the upper mantle of the Earth forces its way up to the surface through cracks in the crust. A volcanic eruption can be spectacular, if deadly, producing fiery fountains and swift-flowing rivers of red-hot lava.

Most volcanoes occur at the edges of colliding plates (see page 15). The lava produced by these volcanoes is thick and does not flow easily. Because of this, pressures can build up inside and lead to explosive eruptions. An example was the eruption of Mount Saint Helens in Washington State in 1980. This eruption removed a huge part of the mountain and gave rise to a vast mushroom cloud of ash, which drifted for hundreds of miles.

Other volcanoes occur well away from plate boundaries at so-called "hot spots" in the Earth's crust. The Hawaiian Islands sit on top of a hot spot and still boast several active and dormant ("sleeping") volcanoes, including Kilauea.

16

▼ A cross-section through a volcano, showing how the red-hot rock forces its way up to the surface. Most of it pours out of a summit crater. This is at the top of the main channel, or conduit, that leads to a reservoir of molten rock in the so-called magma chamber. When repeated eruptions occur, layers of lava and ash build up, creating a cone-shaped mountain.

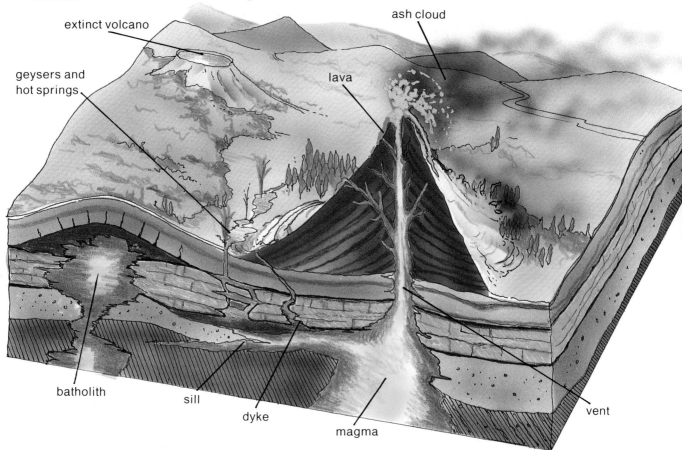

extinct volcano

geysers and hot springs

ash cloud

lava

batholith

sill

dyke

magma

vent

Tremors in the ground

It is no coincidence that earthquakes also occur at the boundaries between plates. The plates constantly push and rub against one another. These movements do not take place smoothly, but in a series of jerks.

The jerks set off vibrations, or shock waves, in the ground, causing it to shake violently. In city areas a major earthquake can cause terrible destruction and loss of life, toppling city buildings like houses made of cards.

The plate boundaries are often marked by visible breaks in the rocks called faults. One famous fault is the San Andreas, which runs along the California coastline. It is part of a fault system that is responsible for the many earthquakes that occur along the West Coast.

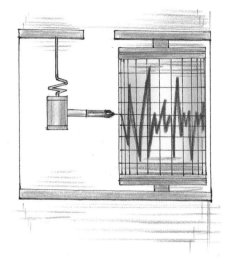

▲ This diagram shows the principle of a seismograph, an instrument that detects earthquakes. The waves set up by an earthquake, called seismic waves, cause the frame of the instrument to shake. The heavy weight suspended on a spring tends to stay still, and the pen it carries makes a trace on the paper on the drum.

Q Fill in the missing word. "The heavy weight tends to stay still because of its ...."

▲ ▶ Molten rock cascades down the slopes of a volcano. It is cooling all the while and will eventually harden into solid lava.

Shaping the land

As soon as mountains are created, either by volcanoes or by the upheavals caused by colliding plates, natural forces begin to destroy them. This process, which is called erosion, is gradual. From year to year, it may not bring about noticeable changes. But over periods of time measured in hundreds, thousands, and millions of years, erosion can bring about dramatic changes to the landscape.

There are many agents of erosion, such as rivers and seas, wind and rain, frost and ice. Of these, running water in rivers perhaps brings about the most noticeable changes. The course of a typical river and the features it creates are followed in the diagram below.

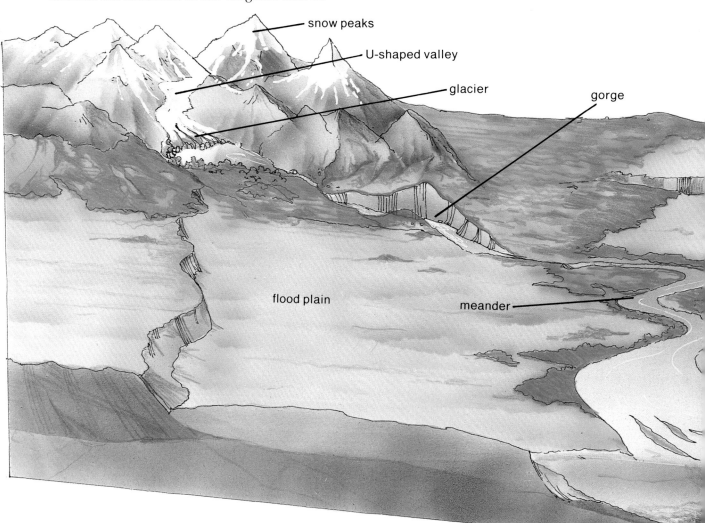

snow peaks

U-shaped valley

glacier

gorge

flood plain

meander

▶ This artificial (false) color picture taken from space shows the huge area of the Mississippi Delta. The Mississippi River carries into the Gulf of Mexico 350 billion gallons (1,300 billion liters) of water a day, containing an enormous amount of sediment. This is deposited when the river meets the sea, creating the huge Delta area.

Q About 500 million tons (450 million tonnes) of sediment are deposited by the river each year. How much deposit on average does each 1,000 gallons 1,000 liters) of river water carry?

Most rivers rise high in a mountain range, where they are fed by high rainfall and melting snows or glaciers. The youthful river runs fast, picking up bits of rock that help it cut into the rocks.

When the river leaves the high ground, it slows down and broadens out. It still causes erosion, but also deposits some of the material it is carrying. The river no longer flows straight, but zigzags from side to side in lazy "meanders." Eventually, the river reaches the sea, where it deposits most of its material as a sediment, which can build up to form an extensive delta region.

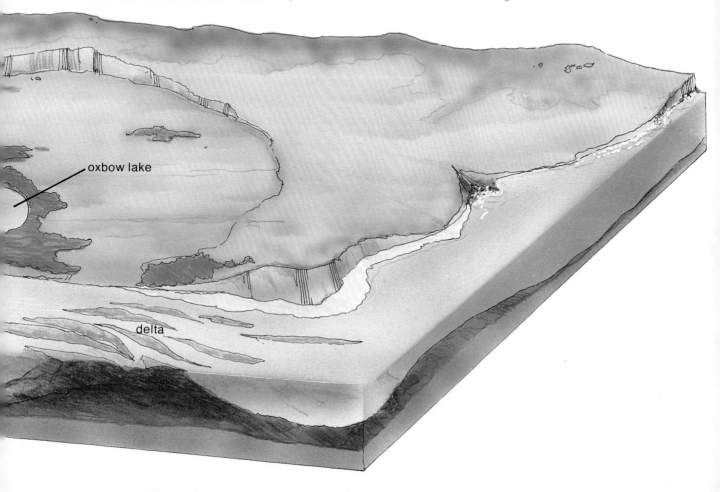

oxbow lake

delta

WORKOUT

The oceans cover 71 percent of the surface of the Earth. Using the figure for the diameter of the Earth you obtained from the Workout on page 11, figure out what the area of the oceans is in square miles (square kilometers).

☆ **Reminder: The area of a sphere of radius r is**
4 × pi × r².

Our watery world

It might be more appropriate if we called our planet "The Water" rather than "The Earth," because water covers more than twice the area of its surface than earth, or land.

Most of this water is contained in the three great oceans – the Pacific, the Atlantic, and the Indian. They have an average depth of about 2½ miles (4 km), but plummet in places to more than 6½ miles (10 km).

In the oceans and the smaller seas dotted around the world, the water is very salty. It is unsuitable for humans and most animals, except fish, to drink. It contains dissolved chemicals called salts, of which the most common is sodium chloride.

Q What is the popular name for sodium chloride?

Fresh water

Only about 2 percent of the water on Earth is fresh and suitable for drinking. This is the water in the rivers and lakes. Another 1 percent of Earth's water is locked in snow and ice, on high mountains, in glaciers, and especially in the ice caps at the North and South Poles.

We and most other living things rely on the 2 percent of fresh water to stay alive. The human body is over two-thirds water. On the average, we drink up to about half a gallon (2 liters) of water a day.

▼ **This map shows the main cool (blue) and warm (red) currents that flow in the oceans of the world. In general, the currents flow clockwise in the Northern Hemisphere, and counterclockwise in the Southern.**

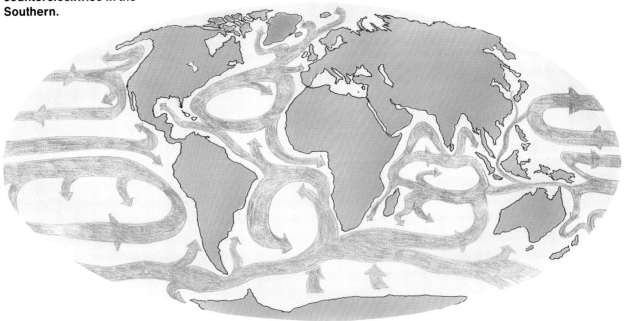

But we use a hundred times this amount of water for other purposes – for bathing, flushing toilets, washing cars, and so forth. Industries use vast amounts of water in chemical processes and especially for cooling purposes. Indeed, the demand for water is threatening to exceed its supply.

Q How much water does your family use in a day? Figure it out roughly by estimating, for example, how many gallon-bucketsful of water you use for various purposes.

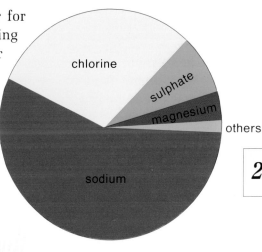

21

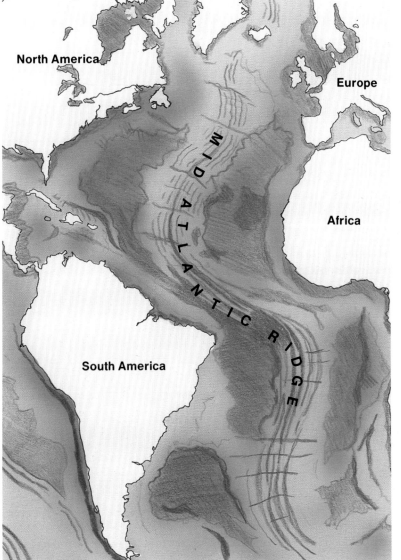

WORKOUT

The pie chart above shows the relative amounts of substances dissolved in seawater. By measurement, find out what percentage there is (A) of sodium; (B) of chlorine. How much more sodium is there than magnesium?

◀ If the Atlantic Ocean dried up, this is what the ocean floor would look like. In the middle is a zigzag chain of rugged mountains, called the Mid-Atlantic Ridge. A similar ridge is found in the other oceans. It shows where new crust is being formed from molten rock welling up from below. The new crust moves away from the ridge on both sides. This process is called ocean-floor spreading.

The atmosphere

To stay alive, we and almost all living things must breathe oxygen. We need oxygen to "burn" the food we eat. We "burn" food in our bodies to produce the energy we need to grow, and move about.

We get our oxygen from the atmosphere, the layer of air that surrounds our planet. This layer is important for other reasons, too. It protects us from harmful radiation coming from the Sun and from outer space in general. It also acts as a blanket to keep the Earth's surface from cooling down too much at night.

The air is a gas, or rather a mixture of gases. The other main gas besides oxygen is nitrogen. A third main gas is called argon, but this makes up just less than one percent of the air. Two other important gases are carbon dioxide and water vapor, which is water in the form of a gas.

The air has weight and presses down on us with considerable force. Although we can't feel it, we support a weight of about 1 ton (900 kg) on our shoulders! On every square inch of our bodies there is a pressure of about 14.7 lb/sq in (1.05 kg/sq cm). This is called the atmospheric pressure.

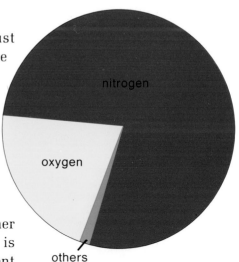

▼ **Sometimes, just before sunset, the skies turn a beautiful reddish-orange. This happens because the Sun is low and its light has to travel through the lower part of the atmosphere, which is sometimes very dusty. The dust lets orange and red light through easily, but tends to block light of short wavelengths, such as blue.**

WORKOUT

The pie chart above shows the main gases found in the air. By measurement, figure out (A) the percentage of oxygen and (B) the ratio of nitrogen to oxygen in the air.

22

► This diagram shows a "block" of atmosphere up to a height of 200 miles (320 km).

Most of the air lies in the lowermost 7 miles (11 km) or so, in a region called the troposphere. This is where most of our weather takes place.

Above the troposphere is the stratosphere. This contains a layer of ozone, a kind of oxygen. The ozone layer helps protects the Earth by filtering ultraviolet light out of sunlight.

Above the stratosphere is a region called the ionosphere. This is so called because the air is present, not as molecules, but as ions, or charged atoms. It is in the ionosphere that displays of aurora occur and meteors burn up.

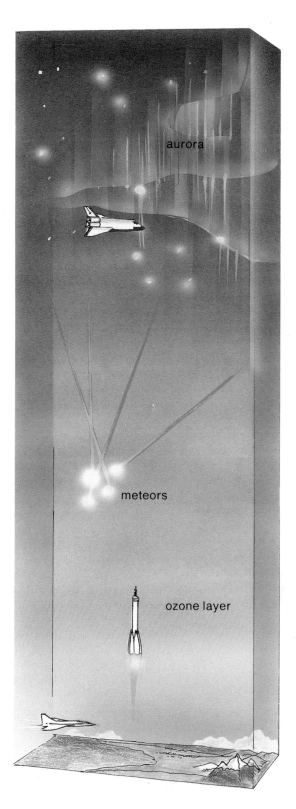

▼ Pictures taken from space show vividly how thin the layer of air around the Earth is. It is thinner relative to the Earth than the peel on an orange.

Birth of the Earth

24

Giant dragonfly

Amphibian

Sea fern

Jelly fish

Brachiopod

Sea Scorpion

Coelecanth-type fish

Sea lily

Ammonite

Trilobite

Starfish

600   550   450   400   350

MILLIONS OF YEARS AGO

WORKOUT

The illustration opposite shows a kind of measuring tape, whose length represents the number of years the Earth has existed. It begins when the Earth was born and ends with the present. The scale on the tape is indicated on the pictorial composition that appears at the bottom of the page.

By measuring the tape with a ruler and using this scale, figure out how old the Earth is.

Age of the Earth

It is only in this century that geologists have figured out how old the Earth is. Hitherto, no one had any idea of its age, although this did not stop them from making wild guesses!

For example, in the 1600s, an Irish Archbishop named Ussher announced that the Earth was created in 4004 BC. This figure was accepted for many years.

In the late 1700s and early 1800s, however, the study of fossils in layers of rock made geologists realize that the Earth must be much older.

They could not figure out how old, but from their studies they were able to calculate relative ages. In other words, they could tell that certain rocks and fossils were younger or older than others.

Since the 1920s, however, geologists have been able to give an actual date to rock formations. They use a method called radiometric dating. It depends on the known rate of decay (breakdown) of certain radioactive substances, such as uranium, that are present in the rocks. This technique has shown that some Earth rocks are billions of years old.

25

▼ Living things did not appear on Earth in any great numbers until about 600 million years ago. The picture shows examples of species that lived at certain times.

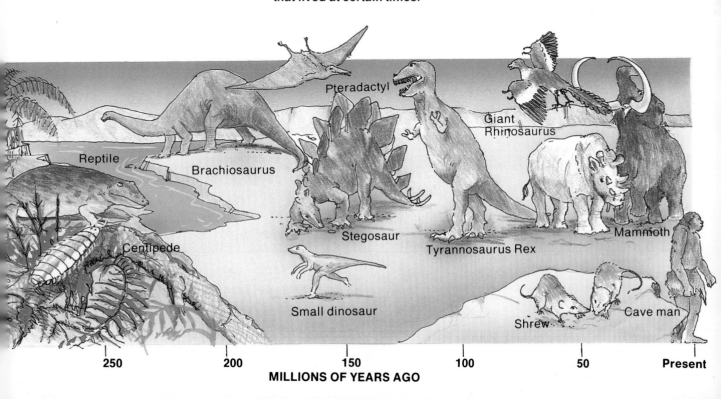

Reptile · Brachiosaurus · Pteradactyl · Stegosaur · Tyrannosaurus Rex · Giant Rhinosaurus · Mammoth · Centipede · Small dinosaur · Shrew · Cave man

2 Mineral Resources

Three main kinds of rocks make up the Earth's crust. Some were born in the lava flowing from fiery volcanoes. Some were formed from layers of sediment washed down by rivers or from chemicals deposited when ancient seas dried up. Others are the piled-up remains, or fossils, of ancient sea creatures.

These rocks are in turn made up of minerals. These are chemical compounds in which the various chemical elements – the basic building blocks of matter – are combined together in fixed proportions.

Many minerals are valuable as raw materials. They may be used as they are, or they may be processed into metals and other useful materials. In most rocks, however, the minerals are mixed together haphazardly, and in this form they are not worth mining.

Minerals are worth mining only when certain natural process have concentrated them. Such mineral deposits may occur on or near the surface, in river beds, and deep under ground. Different mining methods have been developed for each type of location.

◀ This magnificent granite cliff is located in Yosemite National Park in California. It is named El Capitan. Because it is formed of granite, which is very hard wearing, it has stood up to the weather better than the original rocks around it, which have long since worn away.

▼ A scene from the "Gold Rush" days in California. Gold was first discovered at Sutter's Mill in January 1848, and by the following year the "Rush" was well underway.

Q What was the popular name for the miners who took part?

Fire rocks

Two of the most common rocks in the Earth's crust are basalt and granite. They form when red-hot molten rock, or magma, from deep inside the Earth forces its way toward or onto the surface and cools. Such rocks are called igneous, or fire-formed, rocks.

Quick cooling

Magma forces its way onto the Earth's surface at volcanoes. It pours forth as lava and, as it meets the air, quickly cools. The minerals in the lava only have time to grow tiny crystals. This results in what is called a fine-grain rock.

Basalt is an example of a fine-grain rock. Its crystals can often be seen only under a magnifying glass or a microscope. If the lava cools rapidly, no crystals grow at all, resulting in a glassy material called volcanic glass or obsidian. When lava containing a lot of gas cools rapidly, a frothy rock called pumice results.

Slow cooling

Often the molten magma can't force itself out onto the ground, but becomes trapped underneath the surface. There it takes a long time to cool down, and the minerals it contains have plenty of time to grow large crystals.

The result is a coarse-grained rock, such as granite or gabbro. Granites are among the most common types of rocks. Their appearance varies widely, depending on the proportions of the various minerals they contain. The most common minerals are whitish or pinkish feldspar, transparent quartz, and mica, which may be white, black, or colored.

Magma that cools exceptionally slowly underground produces a rock in which the crystals can be huge and measured in yards! Such rocks are called pegmatites.

◀ The summit crater of the volcano Haleakala on Maui, one of the Hawaiian Islands. It is one of the world's largest craters, measuring some 20 miles (32 km) across. The volcano is dormant and last erupted in the 1700s. The crater and slopes of the volcano are covered with thick beds of lava and ash from its many past eruptions.

▼ Pumice is a volcanic rock that is riddled with holes. These are formed by gas forcing its way out when the molten rock cools quickly. Pumice is so light that it usually floats on water.

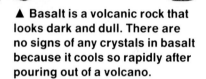

▲ Basalt is a volcanic rock that looks dark and dull. There are no signs of any crystals in basalt because it cools so rapidly after pouring out of a volcano.

▼ Granite is a lighter-colored and much more attractive rock, full of colorful crystals. The specks of mica it contains make it sparkle in the sunlight.

▼ Obsidian is a volcanic rock that is glass-like; it is often called volcanic glass. It forms when molten rock cools very quickly.

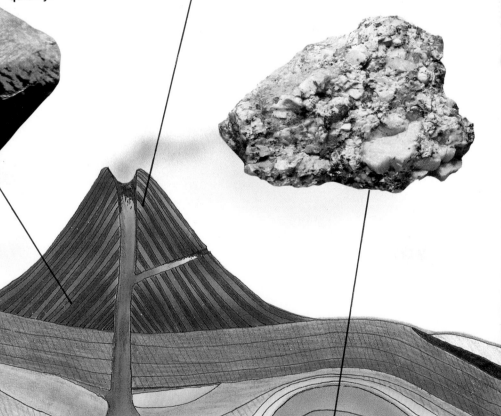

◄ These chalk cliffs were laid down about 100 million years ago, during the Cretaceous Period of Earth's history. ("Cretaceous" comes from the Latin word for chalk.)

▼ This picture shows a section of one of the walls of the Grand Canyon. It shows clearly the different layers of rock formed from sediments that were laid down hundreds of millions of years ago. To the geologist, the various layers of rock are like the pages of a book telling the story of Earth's ancient history.

Sedimentary rocks

The gradual but relentless action of the weather, flowing water, glaciers, and other natural processes will eventually break down even the hardest rocks into tiny particles. Rivers carry away the particles and deposit them as sediments elsewhere.

Over periods of time measured in millions of years, layers of sediment build up and become cemented together to form rock. This type of rock is called sedimentary rock or bedded rock. Often the layers, or strata, can be clearly seen. Typical sedimentary rocks are sandstone formed from layers of sand, and shale formed from layers of mud.

Q Coal is a special kind of sedimentary rock found in layers in ordinary rocks. Why is it special?

In ancient seas

Water flowing over the rocks sometimes dissolves minerals in the rock and carries them into lakes and seas. There they build up. When the water can hold no more, some of the minerals are deposited. If a lake or sea dries up completely, deep beds of minerals may be deposited that in time become rock-hard. This kind of sedimentary rock is called an evaporite. Rock salt and many limestones were formed in this way.

Other limestones consist of the piled-up remains, or fossils, of creatures that lived in ancient seas, such as corals and shellfish. In some of them you can clearly see the fossils. But in others, such as pure white chalk, the fossils are microscopic.

▼ A piece of shale. Millions of years ago, it was part of a mudbank at the estuary of a river. It was changed into solid rock by the enormous pressure of layers of mud above it. Notice the fossil it contains. Shales are rich in fossils of many kinds.

32

◄ Marble is a favorite material for sculpting statues because it is hard, shiny, and weather-resistant. It is a changed form of the soft sedimentary rock limestone.

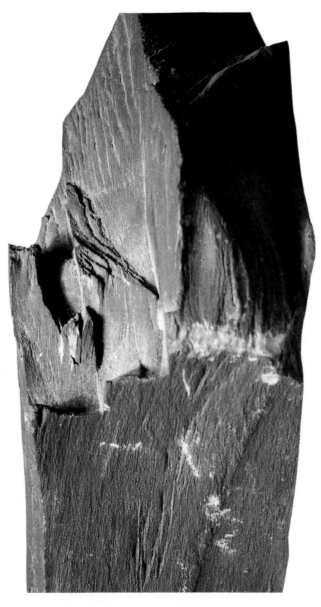

Changed rocks

It is not only rocks on the surface that undergo change as time goes by. Underground rocks can change, too, when they are exposed to heat, or pressure, or both. They change into a new type of rock called metamorphic rock. ("Metamorphic" means "changed form.") Both igneous and sedimentary rocks can change into metamorphic rocks.

The way rocks change varies according to the conditions they are exposed to. New kinds of minerals can appear, for example. Or existing crystals can grow much bigger. Where the pressure is intense, the rocks become very hard, and the minerals they contain may become pressed into bands.

Among common metamorphic rocks are gneiss, marble, slate, and schist. Many specimens of gneiss and schist are studded with a semiprecious stone called garnet.

▲ Slate is a metamorphic rock that formed when shale was exposed to great pressure. The pressure has caused the rock to have a pronounced layered structure. This allows the rock to be split easily into thin sheets.

Q What is a common use for sheets of slate?

Fossils in the rocks

We have seen that some sedimentary rocks are made up of the microscopic remains, or fossils, of tiny sea creatures (see page 31). But much bigger fossils are to be found within sedimentary rocks of all kinds. It is by studying these fossils that we have been able to piece together the history of life on Earth. The study of fossils is called paleontology.

Fossils are the evidence of living things. Whole mammoths, for example, have been found preserved in ice in the Arctic. And insects have been found preserved in amber. But usually living things decay and disappear when they die.

The bodies of some creatures, however, become buried before they decay and leave behind evidence of what they were like.

Sometimes the clay or mud they were buried in hardens. Later their bodies decay or dissolve away, leaving a hollow mold that preserves their outer shape or the shape of their bones. We can find out what they or their bones looked like by making a plaster cast from the mold.

Sometimes the remains of living things are preserved in stone. This happens when water containing minerals slowly dissolves the original remains and replaces them with the minerals. The remains turn into stone, or become petrified.

Q 1. Why are no fossils found in igneous and metamorphic rocks?

▶ Trilobites are some of the most common fossils found. They were one of the earliest successful life forms, well established by the beginning of the Cambrian Period, 590 million years ago.

Q 2. How do you think they got their name?

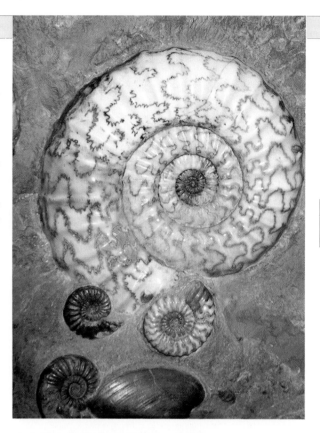

▲ A "family" of ammonites, partly cut out of the rock in which they are embedded. Considering these fossils are millions of years old, they look remarkably fresh, like some of the shells we find on the seashore today.

▲ Crystals show up clearly in this specimen of pyrite, or iron pyrites. Some samples look like gold and are called "fools gold."

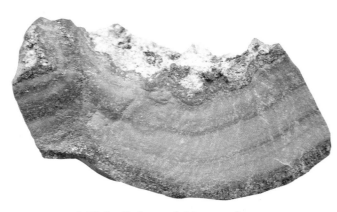

▲ Malacite is a valuble ore of copper.

▼ Lapis lazuri has been valued for its deep blue color for centuries.

Minerals and crystals

Rocks are made of minerals. They are compounds – combinations of certain chemical elements. The most common mineral of all is quartz. It is made up of silicon dioxide, a combination of silicon and oxygen. In the quartz molecule, or basic particle, two atoms of oxygen are combined with one atom of silicon. Quartz, no matter where it is found, always has this exact composition.

Another common mineral, calcite, is calcium carbonate. The calcite molecule is made up of one atom of calcium, one of carbon, and three of oxygen. Again, all samples of calcite always have this exact composition.

Q If Si is the chemical symbol for silicon, Ca for calcium, C for carbon, and O for oxygen, write down the chemical formula for quartz and for calcite.

Crystal shapes

Most rocks are made up of a number of minerals mixed together. We can often see them as different colored crystals. These crystals have no particular shape because they have grown into a compact mass.

But when mineral crystals can grow unhindered, in cavities in the rocks, they take on a characteristic shape. Rock salt crystals, for example, have the shape of a cube. So have fluorite crystals. Calcite and quartz form pointed crystals that resemble sharpened pencils. Epsom salts have crystals like needles.

Every mineral always forms the same shaped crystal. This shape reflects the way the atoms are arranged in the basic crystal structure, or "space lattice." Altogether there are seven different space lattices, and therefore seven different basic crystal shapes.

Q What do sugar and salt have in common? Look at them under a magnifying glass and you will find out.

▼ Of all the crystals in the Earth's crust, none are more prized than diamonds. Diamonds don't look very impressive when they are taken from the ground. Only when they are expertly cut, as here, do they dazzle. They reflect and refract light like no other substance, giving them a unique brilliance and "fire."

INVESTIGATE

Try growing crystals yourself – it isn't difficult. You can grow some good crystals using alum (potassium aluminum sulfate), or detergent made from sodium carbonate, both of which you can get at a drug store.

Add alum or sodium carbonate to a pan of hot water, and stir until the material dissolves. Keep adding alum and stirring until no more alum will dissolve. Let the solution cool a little, then pour it into a jar. Dangle a thread from a pencil so that it touches the surface of the solution. Leave the jar where it can't be disturbed, and look at it every day. You will find that a crystal will start growing on the end of the thread. Notice what shape it is.

Repeat the investigation and grow another crystal. Is it the same shape as the first?

35

Ore minerals

Of all the materials we use in our everyday lives, metals are by far the most important. A few metals can be found in the form of metals in the Earth's crust: gold, silver, and platinum are examples. They are called native metals.

Most metals, however, are found in the ground as chemical compounds, combined with other elements in a variety of different minerals. Usually these minerals are scattered as specks throughout the rocks, and in this form they are not worth mining. It only becomes profitable to mine and process minerals when they occur as concentrated deposits. Then they are called ores.

Ore deposits

Ore deposits may form in a number of ways. Some form when molten rock, or magma, cools underground (see page 28). After most of the rock has become solid, a very runny liquid remains that is rich in minerals. This liquid forces its way through cracks in the rocks and deposits the minerals it contains as rich "veins." Copper, lead, and zinc ores are often found in veins.

▼ **The location of the main regions of the world where the ores of some of our most important metals are found. North America has rich deposits of most of these ores. Iron ore is the one extracted in the greatest quantities, mainly from mines around Lake Superior.**

Q **Why is this lake's name an appropriate one?**

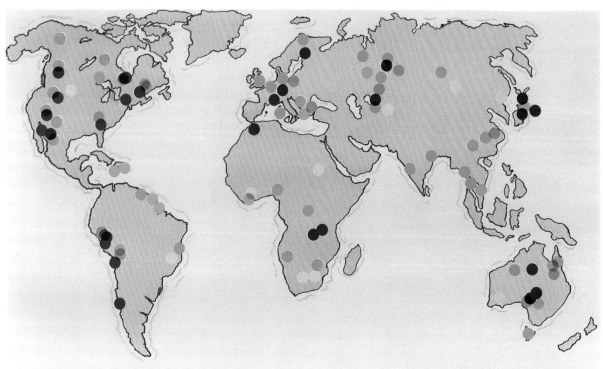

● = zinc ● = aluminum ● = gold ● = silver
● = iron ● = copper ● = tin ● = lead

The action of the weather on surface rocks gradually breaks them down (see page 30). Flowing water may then carry away the minerals they contain and deposit them in a certain place. Gold and heavy minerals such as cassiterite (tin ore) are often found in such deposits, called placers.

Some minerals are dissolved from the rocks by the water flowing over them. The mineral-rich water collects in lakes or seas. Minerals may then be precipitated, or come out of solution. Many iron and copper ores were formed in this way.

Q Why do you think gold, for example, exists in native form and iron doesn't? Why do you think gold is called a precious metal?

▶ **Gold leaf adorns the dome of the State Capitol building in Boston. Gold can be beaten into leaf so thin that it is transparent!**

▶ **Ornate iron balconies in the French Quarter of New Orleans. Most were erected in the 19th century.**

▼ **This rock contains a sample of an iron ore called hematite, a word meaning "blood." It is so named because of its color. Hematite sometimes forms kidney-like masses, and this is then called kidney iron ore.**

Minerals galore

The ores from which we extract our metals are by no means the only useful minerals. There are hundreds more for which we find uses. Let's look at a few interesting ones:

Asbestos: This is a mineral that occurs in rocks in the form of fibers.

Barytes: This is the chalky-white mineral you drink when you have a stomach X-ray. It blocks X-rays and makes the stomach show up.

Iceland spar: This is a form of calcite. When you look at something through it, you see double. This is a property called double refraction.

Calcite: One of the most common of all minerals, this is the main mineral in chalk and limestone. Limestone has a host of industrial uses, for example, in iron smelting and making glass and cement.

China-clay: This is the pure white clay from which the best pottery is made.

Corundum: This is a very hard mineral, used in small grains on abrasive paper. Its pure crystals are fine gems. They are called ruby, emerald, and sapphire, depending on their color.

Cryolite: This mineral has the same refractive index as water. This means that it affects light in exactly the same way as water.

Gypsum: This is a common rock that looks like chalk (calcium carbonate), but is actually another calcium compound (calcium sulfate). Blackboard chalk is made of gypsum. When heated, gypsum turns into plaster of Paris.

Sulfur: This is a chemical element, found native in volcanic regions. It is made into sulfuric acid, the single most important industrial chemical.

Talc: This is one the softest minerals, also called soapstone because it feels "soapy" to the touch.

▼ Even mud has its uses! These mud brick dwellings in New Mexico were built by the Pueblo Indians.

▲ This skyscraper, the Hancock Tower in Boston, has walls made of glass. Glass is a valuable constructional material made largely from the minerals silica (from sand) and lime (from limestone).

38

▶ Tiles made from silica cover many parts of the space shuttle. They are excellent insulators – they glow red-hot when the orbiter returns to Earth but keep the heat from getting to the metal underneath.

Q Why does the outside of the orbiter get hot when it returns to Earth from space?

How hard?

You can help identify a mineral by testing its hardness. Hardness is expressed on a scale on which the softest minerals, such as talc, have a hardness of 1, and the hardest minerals, such as diamond, have a hardness of 10. Field guides on rocks and minerals give information about mineral hardness. Handy tips: If you can scratch a mineral with a fingernail, its hardness is about 2; with a bronze coin, about 3; with glass, about 4, with a penknife, about 6, with flint, about 6, and with a steel file, about 7.

Mining methods

Mining is the oldest industry there is. In early prehistoric times people dug flint out of the ground to make tools and weapons. By about 6,000 years ago, copper ores were being mined and smelted into copper metal. Today mining is a vast industry: mines in the United States produce minerals worth more than $30 billion a year.

Mining takes place both on the surface and deep underground. Surface mining, often called open-pit or strip mining, is relatively simple. It begins by stripping off any dirt, or overburden, over the mineral deposit. This is done by mammoth excavators called "walking draglines." The mineral deposit is then broken up by explosives and loaded into railroad wagons or trucks for removal.

Digging out rock, stone, clay, sand, and gravel at the surface is called quarrying.

Placer mining

Heavy minerals such as gold and tin ore can often be found in placer deposits. These deposits are typically found in the gravel of stream or lake beds and are recovered from the gravel by washing. Miners in the Gold Rush days (see illustration on page 27) used a hand-held pan for washing.

Q What was this method of mining called?

◀ **Tin mining in Malaysia, in Southeast Asia. The tin ore, cassiterite, is found in the gravel in lake and river beds. It is extracted by huge floating dredgers, which can dredge and process tens of thousands of tons of gravel a day.**

Underground mining

Mining minerals underground is a more expensive, difficult, and dangerous operation. Shafts have to be sunk and tunnels dug to reach the minerals, which occur typically in veins in the rocks. If the veins are rich, they may be followed down to great depths. This is what happens in the gold mines of South Africa, some of which are being worked at depths approaching 2 ½ miles (4 km).

A different method of underground mining is used to extract some deposits of halite, or rock salt. Water is pumped down into the deposit through bored holes. It dissolves the salt and returns to the surface.

41

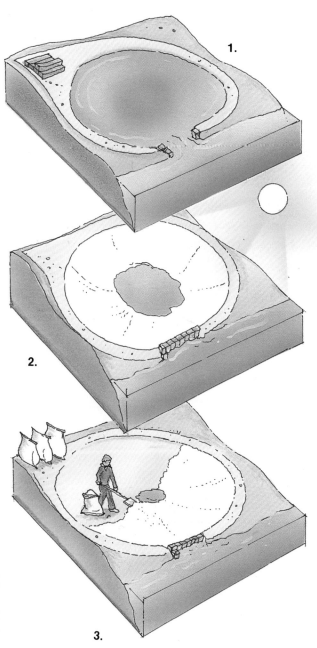

1.

2.

3.

▲ Deep underground, a coal miner checks the operation of a mechanical coal cutter. Mechanical mining is possible because coal is soft and is usually found in thick seams, unlike most ordinary mineral deposits.

▲ This is another kind of surface mining practiced to extract salt from seawater. (1) Seawater is let into a shallow lagoon, or pan. (2) The heat of the Sun evaporates the water. (3) All the water has evaporated, leaving behind the salt it contained.

Q If a deep lagoon was used in the operation, more salt would be obtained. What would be the drawback?

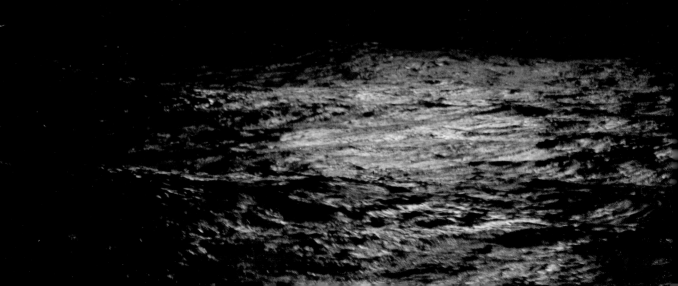

3 Energy Resources

◀◀ **Offshore oil-production rigs, with gas being burned off. Rich offshore oil fields are now being worked in many parts of the world. New technologies have had to be developed to cope with deep-water operations.**

From the moment we get up in the morning until the time we go to bed at night, we are using up some of Earth's precious energy resources.

We use up these resources directly, for example, by burning gas on a gas stove. We also use up energy indirectly, if we throw away a soda can. We have used up the energy that was needed first to mine the ore, then to extract the metal from it, and finally to shape the metal into a can.

The fuels we use in the greatest quantities are coal, oil, and natural gas. We call them fossil fuels because they are the decayed remains of once-living things. The metal uranium is another energy resource; it is used as "fuel" in the reactors of nuclear power stations.

There are limited amounts of all these fuel resources in the Earth's crust, and some day they will run out. To make them last longer, increasing use is now being made of renewable energy resources, such as flowing water, sunshine, and wind.

◀ **A wind turbine being tested at a site in New Mexico. This novel type of "windmill" is called the Darreius. No prizes for guessing why it is nicknamed "the eggbeater!"**

The fossil fuels

Coal, oil, and gas began forming hundreds of millions of years ago. Coal is the remains of plants that grew in humid, swamp-like forests. Oil and gas are the remains of tiny plants and animals that teemed in ancient seas.

Most of the coal seams we find today were laid down between about 290 and 360 million years ago during the Carboniferous Period of Earth's history. In the forests that flourished then grew huge, tree-like ferns and giant horse-tails. When they died, they fell into the swamp and started to decay, or rot down, and eventually turned into a peat-like material.

Over the years, layers of peaty material piled up. From time to time the layers became covered by sand or mud. Over millions of these years they were changed by heat and pressures in the Earth's crust into the hard "mineral" we call coal.

Q In the ancient swampy forests, the main animal life consisted of creatures that could live both in the water and on the land. What do we call this class of creature?

▼ **This map shows the main regions of the world where fossil fuels are found. North America is blessed with abundant supplies of all three fuels.**

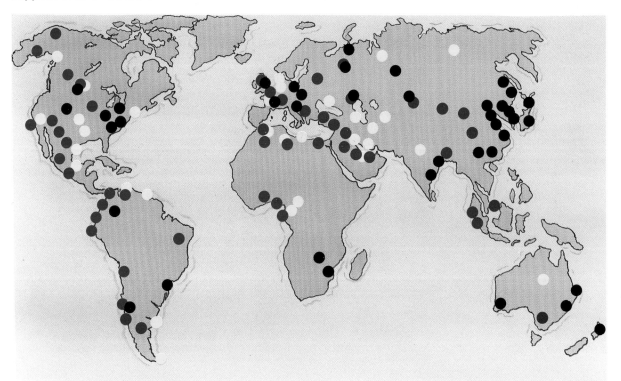

● = Oil   ● = Gas   ● = Coal

44

Oil and gas

Oil and natural gas have their origin in the minute organisms that floated and swam in ancient seas. They were similar to the algae and plankton that live in the oceans today.

When the organisms died, their bodies slowly sank and settled on the seabed. There they formed a kind of slimy ooze, which then became covered with sand and mud. Over many years the ooze was broken down by the action of bacteria and later "cooked" by heat in the crust. It changed into the black liquid we know as oil.

Being a liquid, the oil was able to travel through holes, or pores, in the rocks until it came up against non-porous rock, where it became trapped. The most common kind of trap is an arch formed by rocks when the crust folded under pressure.

Gas was also produced during the oil-forming process, and it, too, accumulated in traps, sometimes with the oil and sometimes by itself.

Q We usually call the gas that comes from the ground natural gas. Why do we add the word "natural?"

45

This is what the swampy forests of Carboniferous times might have looked like. Giant dragonflies flitted through the trees, while crocodile-like animals lumbered through the undergrowth.

Oil and gas

Oil is now the most important of all the fossil fuels, providing about 40 percent of the world's energy. Natural gas provides about 20 percent. Together they provide about twice as much energy as coal.

As it comes from the ground, oil is a thick, greenish-black liquid. In this form it is called crude oil, or petroleum ("rock oil"). It is a mixture of hundreds of different chemical substances, called hydrocarbons because they are made up of hydrogen and carbon.

By itself, this mixture is of little use. Only when it is

▲ A scene at Titusville, Pennsylvania, in about 1860, showing where a retired railroad worker named Edwin Drake dug the first oil well.

46

Location of the main oilfields in North America. The United States annual oil production is about 2.7 billion barrels, worth about $54 billion.

Q If 1 barrel equals 42 gallons (160 liters), how many gallons (liters) of oil does the United States produce per hour?

processed in a refinery does it become really useful. Oil refinery processes split it up into a number of parts. The most important parts are gasoline, kerosene, diesel, and heating oil. Other parts can be processed into useful industrial chemicals from which plastics, paints, dyes, pesticides, and many other products can be made.

Natural gas is also made up of a mixture of hydrocarbons. The main ones are methane, butane, and propane. Butane and propane are easily separated because they turn into liquid under pressure. In liquid form, they are sold in pressurized containers as "bottled gas."

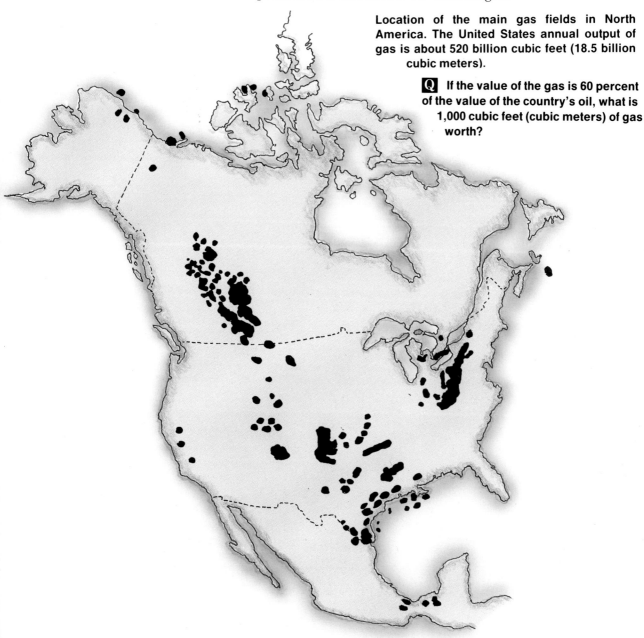

Location of the main gas fields in North America. The United States annual output of gas is about 520 billion cubic feet (18.5 billion cubic meters).

Q If the value of the gas is 60 percent of the value of the country's oil, what is 1,000 cubic feet (cubic meters) of gas worth?

Producing oil

Engineers extract the oil trapped underground through holes they drill down through the rocks. But first they have to find it!

Prospecting (looking) for oil is the work of oil geologists. They look for likely rock formations, using aerial photographs and satellite images. Then they carry out a seismic survey, which involves bouncing sound waves from the underground rocks. From the echoes they receive back, they can plot the rock structure. This work may reveal a possible oil trap.

Next they set up an oil rig and start test drilling. The drilling is done by means of a toothed drill bit on the end of a long string of pipes. New lengths of pipe are added as drilling proceeds. The borehole is also usually lined with steel tubes as it deepens.

A special mud is pumped down the drill pipes. This helps lubricate the bit and flush back to the surface pieces of cut rock. If oil is found, the hole in the ground becomes an oil well. The borehole is capped with a set of control valves known as a Christmas tree.

INVESTIGATE

Which is lightest, oil or water? Pour some oil and water into a jar and see what happens. Stir the oil and water mixture vigorously. Does oil dissolve in water?

◄ An oil-drilling rig on the North Slope of Alaska, where oil was discovered in 1968. The rig is enclosed to offer workers protection from temperatures that can plummet to below −60°F (−50°C).

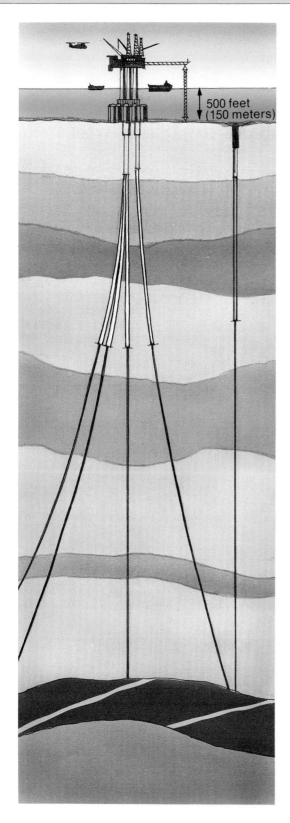

500 feet
(150 meters)

In recent years, oil prospectors have widened their search for oil considerably and have been particularly successful offshore. Offshore drilling and production in deep and inhospitable waters have provided the biggest challenges yet to oil engineers.

Just think of the problems involved in drilling. While gales may blow and temperatures may drop below freezing, prospectors must drop a string of pipes several hundred feet to a precise point on the seabed and then try to drill through thousands of feet of hard rock in the hope – just a hope – that they might hit a lucky strike!

◀ **This diagram shows to scale an offshore oil operation. The oil is extracted through pipes drilled from a production platform on the seabed. The pipes are angled out to reach different parts of the oil reservoir.**

Q **If the depth of the sea in this operation is 500 feet (150 meters), how far down is the oil?**

▼ **An offshore oil complex in Abu Dhabi in the Persian Gulf. It includes not only a production platform, but also an accommodation platform for the operating crew. The Persian Gulf is the richest oil-producing region in the world, with Saudi Arabia, Iraq, Iran, and Kuwait being major producing countries.**

Coal

The remains of plant life that turned into coal (see page 44) were exposed to different amounts of heat and pressure for different amounts of time. This has resulted in there being several grades of coal. They vary mainly in the amounts of carbon and moisture they contain.

Coal that has been subjected to the least heat and pressure is soft and brownish in color. It contains a lot of moisture and only about 50 percent carbon. It is called lignite, or brown coal. When this material was exposed to increased heat and pressure, it turned into bituminous

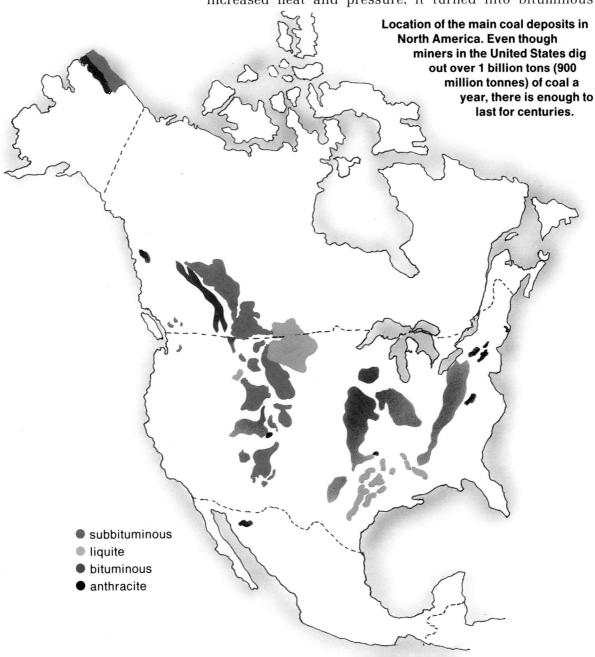

Location of the main coal deposits in North America. Even though miners in the United States dig out over 1 billion tons (900 million tonnes) of coal a year, there is enough to last for centuries.

- ● subbituminous
- ● liquite
- ● bituminous
- ● anthracite

coal. Bituminous coal is much harder, has less moisture, and is nearly 90 percent carbon.

Exceptionally high pressures turned bituminous-type coals into anthracite. This is very hard, has only traces of moisture, and is nearly pure carbon. It burns with a blue, nearly smokeless flame.

Q Some coal also contains traces of sulfur. When it burns, the sulfur escapes into the air as sulfur dioxide. So much of this gas is now getting into the air that it is causing a serious environmental problem. What problem is this?

Coke and gas

Large amounts of coal are burned in power stations. But even larger amounts are used in the iron and steel industry, in the form of coke. Coke is used as fuel in blast furnaces.

Coke is made by heating coal out of contact with the air at temperatures of up to 2,200°F (1,200°C). The gas given off in the process is a useful fuel because it contains hydrogen, methane, and carbon monoxide.

▲ **A piece of anthracite. This shiny black coal is hard and clean to the touch, unlike other types of coal. In the United States most anthracite is mined in the Pennsylvanian coalfields.**

▼ **This fearsome piece of equipment is called a continuous miner. Its rotating, spike-carrying heads cut out the coal from the coalface. The coal falls onto a conveyor underneath, which carries it to the rear and feeds it to a wagon or another conveyor.**

Nuclear energy

On December 2, 1942, at the University of Chicago, a new kind of energy was harnessed for the first time. It was nuclear energy – energy that comes from the nucleus, or center, of atoms.

The atoms of most chemical elements are stable – they never change. But the atoms of some elements are unstable. Under certain conditions, these atoms can be made to split up, a process known as fission. When fission takes place, large amounts of energy are released.

Nuclear fission is the energy-producing process that takes place in nuclear power stations. The atoms that are split are atoms of a heavy metal called uranium. In a power station, the uranium "fuel" is contained in a

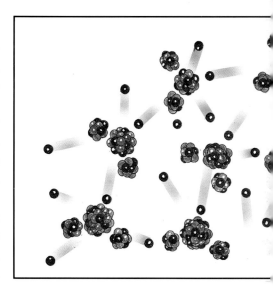

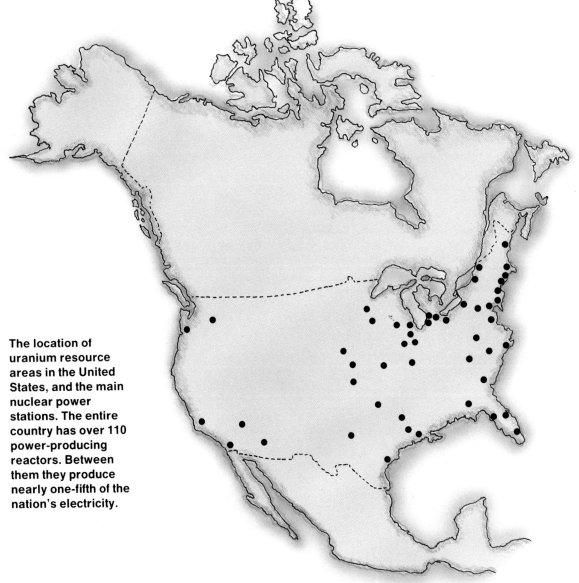

The location of uranium resource areas in the United States, and the main nuclear power stations. The entire country has over 110 power-producing reactors. Between them they produce nearly one-fifth of the nation's electricity.

Chain reaction

A uranium atom splits when it is bombarded by an atomic particle called a neutron. During splitting, or fission, energy is given out and two or more neutrons are released. These may then go on to split other uranium atoms, with the release of even more energy. The splitting of these atoms gives rise to still more neutrons, which go on to split still more atoms and release still more energy. This process in which the splitting of one atom triggers off the splitting of others is called a chain reaction. It holds the key to nuclear energy.

so-called reactor. A cooling liquid, or coolant, circulates through the reactor to carry away the heat produced by fission.

The fission process must be very carefully controlled. If it were allowed to go too fast, a devastating explosion would result, like that produced by nuclear weapons. So the reactor is fitted with control rods that are pushed in or pulled out to keep fission under control. In an emergency, they are pushed all the way in, and this shuts the reactor down.

Reactor design

The diagram at the left outlines the design of the most common type of nuclear reactor. It is called a pressurized water reactor (PWR) because it uses water under pressure as the coolant.

The water is pumped through the uranium core, where it absorbs the heat produced by fission. It passes into a steam generator, where it boils water into steam. The steam is then fed to steam turbines that spin the electricity generators.

Fission produces waste materials that are highly radioactive. This means they give off dangerous radiation that is very harmful to living things. For this reason, the reactor unit is enclosed within a so-called biological shield. This chamber has thick, reinforced concrete walls that block radiation.

▼ Diagram showing the essential features of a pressurized water reactor. Water under pressure extracts the heat from the reactor core.

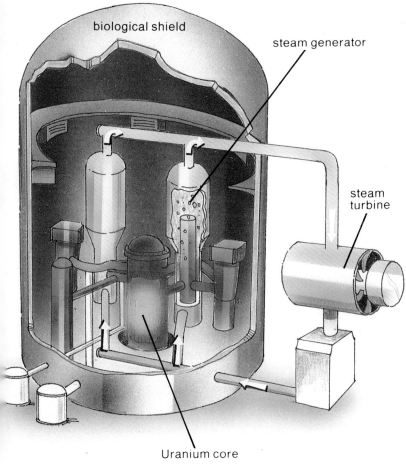

biological shield

steam generator

steam turbine

Uranium core

Renewable resources

We are using up our supplies of fossil fuels at a colossal rate. The world pumps billions of barrels of oil and trillions of cubic feet of natural gas out of the ground each year and digs out billions of tons of coal. These fuels have taken hundreds of millions of years to form, and when they are gone they cannot be replaced. We call them expendable resources. Uranium, the "fuel" that provides nuclear energy, is an expendable resource, too.

In the future, we shall have to make better use of the Earth's renewable resources – those that replenish themselves naturally. These resources include flowing water, sunshine, and wind. Heat locked in underground rocks, or geothermal energy, is another useful renewable resource.

54

▼ Outline of a typical hydroelectric power station. A river valley has been dammed so as to create an artificial lake behind it. Water flows into the turbines and spins them around, turning the electricity generators mounted above.

Q (A) What do we call an artificial lake? (B) Why is the powerhouse located at the bottom of the dam and not at the top?

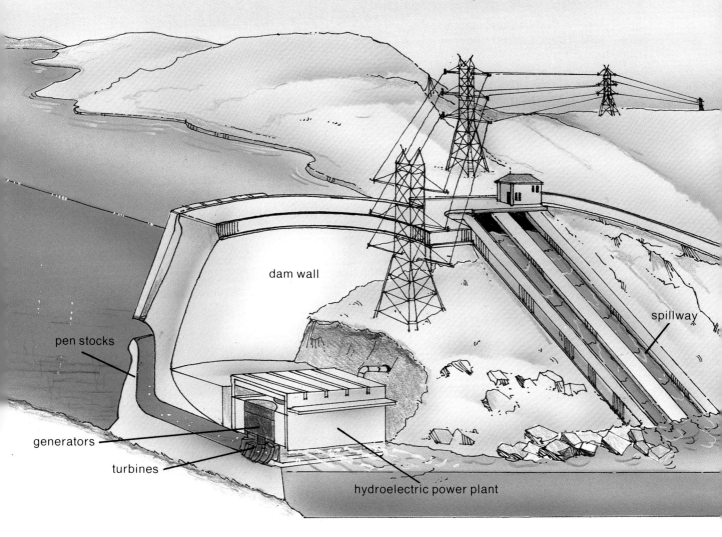

dam wall

pen stocks

spillway

generators

turbines

hydroelectric power plant

We already harness the energy of flowing water on a large scale in hydroelectric power (HEP) stations. The United States has some of the world's most productive HEP stations, the leading one being the Grand Coulee in Washington State, with a power output up to 10,000 megawatts.

Q **1.** How many 100-watt light bulbs could be lit by this HEP station?

Sun power

The Sun bathes the Earth in tens of thousands of times more energy than we will ever need. Much of it goes into driving our weather system, evaporating water from the seas, and driving the winds. We can harness solar power directly, using devices such as solar cells and solar panels, and on a larger scale in "power tower" projects (see below).

We can also harness solar power indirectly by tapping the energy blowing in the wind, using wind turbines. It is estimated that wind power could provide as much as one-tenth of America's energy.

A "fish-eye" view of an experimental solar power tower scheme in New Mexico. Groups of mirrors ring a tall tower and focus sunlight onto it. This concentrated sunlight heats up a boiler, providing steam to drive electricity generators.

Q **2. Why is New Mexico a good location for carrying out solar energy experiments?**

Milestones

MYA means millions of years ago. "Eras," "Periods" and "Epochs" refer to time spans in the Earth's geological history)

4,600 MYA The Earth was born, along with the Sun and the rest of the Solar System. The molten surface cooled to form a hard, rocky crust.

4,600-590 MYA Precambrian times, divided into the two eras (or eons).

4,600-2,500 MYA Archaean Era: the very ancient era. Time of formation of "basement" rocks, mountain-building, and some deposits of sediments.

2,500-590 MYA Proterozoic Era: the era of first life. Time during which life developed in comparative abundance in the seas, although extensive mountain-building and reworking of the Earth's crust eliminated most of the fossils that provide evidence of life.

590-248 MYA Paleozoic Era: the era of ancient life, divided into six periods.

590-505 MYA Cambrian Period: oxygen began to build up in the atmosphere, probably ozone too, allowing life to flourish; the land mass that is now North America was repeatedly flooded.

504-438 MYA Ordovician Period: flooding of continental land masses continued, giving rise to extensive deposits of sediments.

437-408 MYA Silurian Period: at the beginning of the period the Earth was gripped in an ice age, and glaciers covered large regions; later, seas flooded the land.

407-360 MYA Devonian Period: shallow seas still covered most of the continents; land masses collided, giving rise to mountain- building.

359-286 MYA Carboniferous Period: swampy forests covered much of the land, giving rise to the world's great coal seams.

285-248 MYA Permian Period: the world's land masses came together to create the supercontinent Pangaea; extensive mountain-building.

247-65 MYA Mesozoic Era: the era of middle life, divided into three periods.

247-213 MYA Triassic Period: Pangaea remained intact; some volcanic activity.

212-144 MYA Jurassic Period: Pangaea split up and the Atlantic Ocean began to form; extensive sedimentation.

143-65 MYA Cretaceous Period: widespread flooding of the continents, followed by build-up of sediments, particularly chalk.

64-PRESENT DAY Cenozoic Era, the era of recent life, divided into two periods.

64-2 MYA Tertiary Period, divided into five "epochs."

64-55 MYA Paleocene Epoch: mountain- building continued.

54-38 MYA Eocene Epoch: North America separated from Europe; Australia from Antarctica.

37-25 MYA Oligocene Epoch: India collided with Asia, triggering formation of the Himalaya Mountains.

24-5 MYA Miocene Epoch: the Alps began to rise as Africa pressed against Europe; in North America the Sierra Nevada and Rocky Mountains began to form.

4-2 MYA Pliocene Epoch: mountains continued to rise; the climate cooled dramatically, and glaciers began to advance in the far north.

2 MYA – PRESENT DAY Quaternary period, divided into two epochs.

2 MYA – 10,000 YEARS AGO Pleistocene Epoch: time of repeated ice ages, with glaciers covering vast areas of North America and Europe.

10,000 YEARS AGO – PRESENT DAY Holocene Epoch: glaciers retreated to the polar regions at the beginning of the epoch as the climate warmed; humans began to alter the landscape and plunder its resources, particularly from about 200 years ago, when the Industrial Revolution began.

Glossary

AMBER Fossil resin, which sometimes traps within it perfectly preserved insects.

AMMONITE An animal that lived in ancient seas, rather like an octopus in a coiled shell.

ASBESTOS A mineral that occurs naturally in the form of fibers.

ATMOSPHERE The layer of gases that surrounds the Earth.

ATMOSPHERIC PRESSURE The pressure caused by the weight of the atmosphere.

BARREL The unit used to measure the volume of oil. One barrel equals 42 gallons (160 liters).

BASALT One of the most common igneous rocks, which formed on the Earth's surface and has only microscopic crystals.

BIOGENIC A term that describes a sedimentary rock made up of the fossils of ancient creatures.

BOTTLED GAS Properly called liquefied petroleum gas, or LPG; gas extracted from natural gas that turns readily into liquid under pressure.

CENOZOIC ERA The era of recent life; the period of geological time from about 64 million years ago to the present day.

CONTINENTAL DRIFT The gradual movement of the land masses of the Earth because of movements of the plates of the crust.

COAL A fossil fuel, formed from the remains of plants.

CORE The innermost part of the Earth, made of metal.

CRUST The hard, rocky outermost part of the Earth.

CRYSTAL The state most minerals take when they form slowly from molten rock.

EROSION The wearing away of the Earth's surface due to the action of the weather, rivers, glaciers, and so forth.

FAULT A crack in the Earth's crust, often caused by the movement of the crustal plates.

FISSURE A gap in the rock layers.

FLOTATION A common method of mineral dressing (see definition below) in which finely divided mineral particles are separated by floating away in a frothing liquid.

FOLD A bend in the rock layers.

FOSSIL The remains or impressions in the rocks of animals or plants that lived long ago.

GANGUE The rocky and earthy impurities mined with an ore.

GEM A precious stone.

GEOLOGY The study of the Earth and its surface, its origins, and the way it has changed through the ages.

GLACIER A mass of ice, formed of compacted snow, that moves slowly along a river valley.

GRANITE One of the most common igneous rocks, which formed underground. It is made up mainly of crystals of the minerals quartz, feldspar, and mica.

HARDNESS SCALE A scale of 1 to 10 used for determining the hardness of minerals.

HYDROCARBON A chemical made up of hydrogen and carbon only. Petroleum and natural gas are made up almost entirely of hydrocarbons.

HYDROELECTRIC POWER Electricity produced by harnessing the energy of flowing water.

ICE AGE A period when the climate was much colder than it is now and when much of the Earth was covered with sheets of ice.

IGNEOUS ROCK A "fire-formed" rock; one that formed from molten magma, either on the surface or under the surface.

IONOSPHERE The upper layer of the Earth's atmosphere, in which gases are present as ions, or charged atoms.

LAVA Molten rock that flows out of a volcano and that cools and solidifies on the surface.

LITHOSPHERE The solid part of the Earth's surface, the crust and the upper part of the mantle.

MAGMA Molten rock underneath the surface.

MANTLE The rocky material that lies between the Earth's core and crust. It is mostly relatively soft.

MESOZOIC ERA The era of middle life. The period of Earth's history between about 247-65 million years ago.

METAMORPHIC ROCK A changed rock; existing rock that has been changed in form and sometimes in composition by heat and/or pressure inside the Earth's crust.

MINERAL A chemical compound found in the Earth's crust. Every mineral has a definite composition and characteristic chemical and physical properties.

MINERAL DRESSING Readying an ore before smelting, usually by removing unwanted earthy wastes.

NATIVE ELEMENT One that is found in its pure state in the Earth's crust.

NATURAL GAS A fossil fuel, which is the altered remains of tiny organisms that lived in ancient seas.

NUCLEAR ENERGY Energy obtained by splitting the nuclei (centers) of atoms, a process known as fission.

NUGGET A lump of native metal, such as silver or gold.

OIL See PETROLEUM.

OPEN-PIT MINING Mining minerals from a hole at the surface.

ORE A mineral from which metal can be profitably extracted.

OXYGEN The gas in the air that all living things must breathe to stay alive.

OVERBURDEN The soil above a mineral deposit that is removed in surface mining operations.

OZONE LAYER A layer of the Earth's atmosphere that contains a high proportion of ozone, a form of oxygen.

PALEONTOLOGY The study of fossils.

PALEOZOIC ERA The era of ancient life. The period of Earth's history between about 590 and 248 million years ago.

PANNING A method of mining gold practised by early prospectors, in which they swirled around a mixture of water and gravel in a pan.

PETROCHEMICALS Chemicals obtained

by processing petroleum in a refinery.

PETROLEUM Also called crude oil; a fossil fuel, being the altered remains of tiny organisms that lived in ancient seas.

PLACER DEPOSITS Minerals that have been deposited as a result of the action of flowing water.

PLATES Sections of the Earth's crust that are slowly moving, being carried along by currents in the upper mantle.

PLATE TECTONICS The science concerned with the movement of the Earth's crustal plates and its effects, such as sea-floor spreading and mountain-building.

PROSPECTOR A person who looks for minerals and other resources.

QUARTZ The most common mineral on Earth, being the chemical silicon dioxide.

RADIOACTIVE Giving out radiation.

REACTOR A unit in which nuclear energy is extracted at a nuclear power station.

RECYCLING Processing waste materials so that they can be used again.

REFINERY A chemical plant in which petroleum is processed.

RENEWABLE RESOURCES Resources like flowing water and wind that can be used again and again and will not run out.

RESERVOIR An artificial lake.

RIFT VALLEY A valley produced usually when a section of rock sinks between two faults.

ROCK Solid material that makes up the Earth's crust. Rocks are composed of one or more minerals.

SALT A mineral dissolved in seawater, in particular the mineral sodium chloride, common salt.

SEA-FLOOR SPREADING The gradual movement of the ocean floor away from the ocean ridge, where new crustal material is being formed.

SEDIMENT Loose rocky material that has been deposited, usually by flowing water.

SEDIMENTARY ROCK Rock formed from layers of sediment that have over millions of years become compacted and hardened by pressure in the Earth's crust.

SEISMOGRAPH An instrument that detects and measures the strength of earthquakes.

SILICATE One of the most common types of minerals, containing silicon and oxygen combined with certain metals, particularly sodium, potassium, and aluminum.

SMELTING Heating an ore strongly in a furnace, often with other materials, so as to reduce it to metal.

SOLAR ENERGY Energy from the Sun

SPACE LATTICE The basic structure of a crystal.

STRATOSPHERE The layer of the Earth's atmosphere between the troposphere and the ionosphere.

TROPOSPHERE The lowest layer of the Earth's atmosphere.

VEIN A layer of minerals that formed in fissures in existing rocks.

VOLCANO An opening in the Earth's crust through which molten rock, ash, and gases are expelled.

59

60

Page 9
1. Africa is on the left of the picture.
2. Water covers more than twice the area of the land.
3. (A) 24 hours, (B) 365 days.

Page 10
1. Bits of matter are attracted to one another because of gravity.
2. Each lump of matter was traveling fast, with kinetic energy, the energy of motion. When it collided, this energy was converted to heat energy.

Page 11
The diameter of the Earth is 7,926 miles (12,756 km).

Workout
(Volume of a sphere is $4/3 \times pi \times r^3$.)
The volume of the Earth is about 260 billion cubic miles (1,090 billion cubic km). The mass of the Earth is about 6,500 million million million tons (5,900 million million million tonnes).

Page 14
1. The highest Himalayan peak is Mt. Everest, which is about 5½ miles (8.9 km) high.
2. The highest peak in North America is Mt. McKinley.

Page 15
The highest peak in the Appalachians is Mt. Mitchell, in North Carolina.

Page 17
The heavy weight tends to stay still because of its inertia.

Page 19
1,000 gallons of Mississippi water carries about 8 pounds of sediment. (1,000 liters carries about 1 kg of sediment.)

Page 20
Workout
The surface area of the oceans is about 140 million square miles (363 million sq km).

The popular name for sodium chloride is common salt.

Page 21
On average in the developed countries a person uses as much as 40 gallons (150 liters) a day. Many people in the U.S. use more than this.

Workout
(A) Sodium, about 31 percent (B) Chlorine, about 55 percent. There is about 8 times as much sodium as magnesium.

Page 22
Workout
There is about 21 percent oxygen in the air. The ratio of nitrogen to oxygen in the air is about 3.7 to 1.

Page 24
By measuring the tape, you should find that the age of the Earth is about 4,600 million years.

Page 27
The miners who took part in the Gold Rush were called the "Forty-niners."

Page 30
Coal is a special kind of sedimentary rock because it is the compressed and altered remains of huge plants. In other words, it is an organic substance, while most other rocks are inorganic.

Page 32
The most common use for sheets of slate is for roofing houses.

Page 33
1. No fossils are found in igneous rocks because these rocks were formed from molten magma. No fossils are usually found in metamorphic rocks because they have been subjected to heat and pressure, which would have obliterated any fossils.
2. Trilobites got their name because of the distinctive three-part form of their skeleton.

Page 34

The chemical formula for quartz is SiO_2, and the chemical formula for calcite is $CaCO_3$.

Page 35

Both sugar and salt have crystals shaped like cubes.

Investigate

You will find that the second crystal you grow will have the same shape as the first.

Page 36

Lake Superior's name is appropriate because it is the biggest of the Great Lakes, with a surface area of some 31,820 square miles (82,410 sq km).

Page 37

Gold exists in native form because it does not react readily with other chemical elements. But iron combines with elements much more readily, especially with the oxygen in the air.

Page 39

The outside of the orbiter gets hot because of friction with the air.

Quick Quiz

(A) Being a rocky material, asbestos is fireproof.

(B) When it is refracted, a beam of light bends.

(C) Ruby is red, emerald is green, and sapphire is blue.

(D) If you dropped a piece of cryolite into water, it would disappear from sight.

(E) Plaster of Paris is used in medicine for making plaster casts to set broken bones.

(F) Talc is the mineral in talcum powder, used for sprinkling onto babies' skin.

Page 40

Using a pan in placer mining was called panning.

Page 41

If the lagoon were deep, it would not heat up as quickly as the shallow one, and it would take much longer to evaporate.

Page 44

We call a creature that can live both on land and in the water an amphibian.

Page 45

We call the gas that comes from the ground natural gas to distinguish it from other kinds of fuel gases that are manufactured, such as coal gas and coke-oven gas.

Page 46

The United States produces about 13 million gallons (49 million liters) of oil an hour.

Page 47

The value of 1,000 cubic feet of gas is about $1.75. (The value of 1,000 cubic meters is about $62.)

Page 48

Investigate

Oil is lighter (less dense) than water and will therefore form a layer on top of it.

Oil does not dissolve in water no matter how well you shake them up together.

Page 49

If the sea is 500 feet (150 meters) deep, the oil is about 9,200 feet (2,800 meters) below the seabed.

Page 51

In the air, sulfur dioxide combines with oxygen and moisture to form sulfuric acid, which falls to Earth as acid rain.

Page 54

(A) We call an artificial lake a reservoir.

(B) The powerhouse is located at the bottom of the dam where the pressure is greatest, so the pressure will spin the turbine.

Page 55

1. 100 million light bulbs could be lit.

2. New Mexico is a good region for solar energy experiments because it experiences so much sunny weather.

For further reading

Blashfield, Jean F. and Black, Wallace.
Too Many People?
Childrens Press, Chicago, IL. 1992.

Earthworks Group Staff.
Fifty Simple Things Kids Can Do to Recycle.
Earthworks, Berkeley, CA. 1991.

Javna, John.
Fifty Simple Things Kids Can Do to Save the Earth.
Andres and McMeel, Kansas City, MO. 1990.

Leggett, Jeremy and Dennis Legget.
Troubled Waters.
Marshall Cavendish, New York. 1992.

Leggett, Jeremy and Dennis Leggett.
Dying Forsts.
Marshall Cavendish, New York. 1992.

Radford, Don.
Earth's Resources.
David and Charles, North Pomfret, VT. 1983.

Squire, C.B.
Heroes of Conservation.
Fleet Press, New York.

Tolan, Sally.
John Muir: Naturalist, Writer, and Guardian of the North American Wilderness.
Gareth Stevens, Milwaukee, WI. 1989.

Ward, Peter.
The Adventures of Charles Darwin: A Story of the Beagle Voyage.
Cambridge University Press, New York. 1986.

Index

Numbers in *italics* refer to illustrations.

Alaska Range 14
Alps 14
amber 57
ammonite *33*, 57
Andes Mountains 14
anthracite 50, *51*
Appalachians 14, 15
argon 22
asbestos 38, 39, 57
Atlantic Ocean 12, 21
atmosphere 11, 57
atmospheric pressure 22, 57

barrel (measure) 46, 57
barytes 38
basalt 28, *29*, 57
biogenic 57
biological shield 53
bituminous coal *50*, 51
bottled gas 47, 57
brown coal 50
butane 47

calcite 34, 35, 38
Cambrian Period 33
carbon dioxide 22
Carboniferous Period 44, 45
cassiterite 40
Cenozoic Era 57
chain reaction 52, 53
chalk 30, 31
China clay 38
continental drift 12, 13, 57
coal *41*, 50, 51, 57
coal gas 51

coal mining *41*, *51*
coke 51
Cordilleras 14, 15
core 11, 57
corundum 38
Cretaceous Period 30
crude oil 46
crust *11*, 57
cryolite 38, 39
crystal 28, 29, *34*, *35*, 57

dam *54*
diamond *35*
Drake, Edwin 46
dredging *40*
drilling *48*, *49*

Earth
    age 24, 25
    atmosphere 22, 23
    birth 10, 11
    life on 24, 25
    structure *11*
earthquakes 12, 17
El Capitan 26, 27
emerald 38, 39
energy resources 43-55
erosion 18, 19, 57
evaporite 31
excavators 54

fault 17, 57
felspar 28
fission 52
fissure 57
flotation 57
fold 57
fossil 25, 27, 31, *33*, 57
fossil fuels 44, 45

gangue 57
garnet 32

gas 44, 45, 46, 47
gem 32, 57
geology 7, 57
glacier *18*, 19, 20, 57
glass 38
gneiss 32
Gold Rush 27
gold leaf *37*
Grand Canyon *30*, *31*
Grand Coulee 55
granite 28, *29*, 57
gypsum 38

Haleakala 28
hardness scale *39*, 57
Hawaiian volcanoes *6*, *7*, 16
hematite 37
Himalayas 14
hydrocarbon 46, 47, 58
hydroelectric power *54*, 55, 58

ice age 58
Iceland spar 38
igneous rock 28, 29, 58
ionosphere *23*, 58

Kilauea 6, 7, 16

lapis lazuri *34*
lava 16, 17, 58
lignite 50
lithosphere 58

magma 16, 17, 28, 58
malachite *34*
mantle *11*, 58
marble *32*
Mauna Kea 6, 7
Mauna Loa 6, 7
meander 19
Mesozoic Era 58

63

metamorphic rock *32*, 58
methane 47
Mid-Atlantic Ridge *21*
mineral 27, 34, 35, 38, 58
mineral resources 26-41
mineral dressing 58
mining 40, *41*
Mississippi Delta 19
mountain building 14
Mt. Saint Helens 16
mud brick 38

native element 58
natural gas 45, 46, 47, 58
nebula 10
nitrogen 22
Northern Hemisphere 9
nuclear energy 52, 53, 58
nuclear fission 52
nuclear power station 52, 53
nuclear reactor 52, *53*
nugget 58

obsidian 28, *29*
ocean currents 20
ocean ridge 14, 21
oil 45, 46, 47, 58
oil production 48, 49
oil refinery 47
offshore oilfield *42*, 43, *49*
open-pit mining 40, 58
ore 36, 37, 58
oxygen 22, 58
overburden 40, 58
ozone layer *23*, 58

paleontology 33, 58
Paleozoic Era 58
Pangaea 13
panning 58
peat 44

pegmatite 28
petrochemicals 58
petroleum 46, 59
placer deposits 37, 40, 59
plaster of Paris 38, 39
plates 12, 13, 14, 17, 59
plate tectonics 59
pressurized water reactor *53*
prospector *48*, 59
propane 47
pumice 28, *29*

quarrying 40
quartz 34, 35, 59

radioactive 25, 53, 59
radiometric dating 25
reactor 52, 53, 59
recycling 59
Red Sea 8, 9
refinery 59
renewable resources 54, 55, 59
reservoir 59
rift valley 59
river 18, 19
rock 59
Rocky Mountains 14, 15
ruby 38, 39

sapphire 38, 39
salt 20, 21, 59
salt mining *41*
San Andreas fault 17
sandstone 30
schist 32
sea-floor spreading 59
sediment 19, 27, 30, 31, 59
sedimentary rock 30, 31, 59
seismic survey 48
seismograph 17, 59

shale 30, *31*, 32
Sierra Nevada 14, 15
silica 34, 39
silicate 59
slate *32*
smelting 59
soapstone 38
solar energy *55*, 59
solar power tower *55*
Solar System 9, 10
Southern Hemisphere 9
space lattice 59
space shuttle tiles *39*
stratosphere 23, 59
sulphur 38
Sun 9, 10

talc 38, 39
trilobite *33*
troposphere 23, 59

underground mining *41*
uranium 43, 52, 53

vein 36, 59
volcanic glass 28, *29*
volcano 6, 7, 12, *16*, 59

water 20, 21
Wegener, Alfred 12
wind turbine *43*, 55